FLIPSIDE OF
MANAGEMENT
7 FUNNY TALES

Sanjeev Sharan

INDIA · SINGAPORE · MALAYSIA

Notion Press

Old No. 38, New No. 6
McNichols Road, Chetpet
Chennai - 600 031

First Published by Notion Press 2019
Copyright © Sanjeev Sharan 2019
All Rights Reserved.

ISBN 978-1-64587-139-2

Dedication

Dedicated to my late parents, Neela Sharan and Prem Rang Bihari Sharan.

You are always with us.

Contents

Foreword   7

Preface   9

Acknowledgements   11

1. Touch Matters   13

2. Is It CSR or a Branding Opportunity
    @ My Lala Company!!!!   21

3. Performance Management or Relationship Management?   31

4. Recruiting the Right Match or Ego Match?   37

5. Am I a Business President or a President – Sales?   45

6. The Blind Men and the Elephant   53

7. Farmers Appointed as Military Commanders   59

Foreword

People are the greatest asset in any organization. And they will remain so till humans are subjugated to machines though AI. The human beings participate in the organisational process actively unlike other resources who participate passively. This distinguishes people from other resources. Hence it is extremely important to recruit right kind of people, appraise them in a transparent and fair manner and reward them for their performance in order to keep people motivated for the peak performance. In practice many of the organizations lack seriousness in this aspect of people management. *This book by Sanjeev beautifully captures the important dimensions of people management through case studies, I am sure the budding HR managers as well as practioners will find this book by Sanjeev interesting and fruitful.*

– Anirudh Singh

Senior HR Professional (Ex Head HR JSW Steel, Idea)

I started my professional journey from a IT support professional, to IT and Industrial sales, after an hazardous accident I have to shift to a profession with less travel and field work, so have to rebuild my professional life and I started as a computer teacher, and then after as a media professional.

So many of us has a similar incredible journeys that we have been through with many ups and downs. And also have to deal with many situations that teaches us a lot. *If you are a working professional, you can clearly relate to this book, what I like about the author that he has perfectly and wonderfully crafted this book with key topics which is honest and hard-hitting, maybe sometimes funny to read.*

– Jayanta Ghosh

Columnist

After working in different geographies across globe, I believe that the success of any organization depends a lot on its employees and talent people. Organization and Management has the ability to pump in any kind of resources, technology, finance etc but can not create the passion to succeed. During my career I have observed that fairness to the employees has no alternative. It is one of the most powerful tool to connect with people. Sanjeev in his book " Flipside of Management" 7 funny tales" has captured serious aspects of human management and its impact on business in a funny and at times satirical way. These are presented in simple and very easy to relate to. This is worth reading by the business heads as well as aspiring entrepreneurs and professionals across industry to help them understand these softer but very important aspects. I am sure he will continue with his effort of "eye opening" in future also.

– Peng Aiguang

CEO ZTE Telecom India

Preface

*F*lipside of Management is a collection of rib-tickling fictional stories related to one's professional life. It is easy to read. Any professional, either from an MNC or a lala organisation, can relate to it in their day-to-day life. Each story will make the reader feel, "Yes, yes, yes. Aisa hota hai (It happens)." The author focusses on the "reality taste" and has refrained from giving gyan on "Right" or "Wrong". The efforts convey the message purely through facts. It has been left to the reader to interpret and conclude.

The whole reading journey covers some interesting areas such as: a) Recruitment experience of a candidate, b) Relationship-and-emotion-based performance evaluation, c) Neglecting non-sales functions in rewards and recognition events d) Misusing and mixing CSR with branding, e) Short-sighted selection and f) Perception-based management instead of fact-based. The tone is kept simple and easy to understand.

The recruitment story revolves around the interesting experience of a candidate. How the behaviour of an interviewer impacts the image of an organisation's culture in the minds of the candidates.

The CSR story touches on the short circuiting of CSR ethics. It talks about how a few organisations consider CSR spending to be branding opportunities and try to derive image branding out of CSR. The concept of social contribution is overtaken by "What's there for me?"

The next story touches upon the subject of performance evaluation. It talks about how the Performance Management system is tweaked to accommodate favourites. It is interesting to read about how, at times, the PMS (Performance Management system) is misused as a tool for penalising or rewarding, instead of being a development and correction tool.

The pain-point areas of selection are covered interestingly in another story where it highlights how short circuiting of the process overshadows the right spirit of selection. In one of the chapters, the different facets of management are covered. How the leader's softness or bias towards certain functions impacts the overall organisation's culture and motivation. It, at times, creates an invisible "division" within the team. The story highlights the important area of "expectations from a leader."

The last two stories speak about the subject of "looking at the bigger picture" – broadening of vision.

It is sad to find how a few organisations are ignoring the critical competency of "ability to handle a larger role" in the blind race of promoting internal candidates.

*I am sure that after going through the **Flipside of Management,** each one of us will certainly get some food for thought resulting in deeper humane positivity towards people and business.*

Thanks for sparing your time. I will be looking forward to your feedback on my email id sanjusarthak@rediffmail.com

Acknowledgements

This book is not complete without thanking the people who have directly or indirectly motivated me to write. Though there was always an urge to write a book since the last few years and I had even started scribbling during my China stay, the final push came from Anjali (Co-founder of Saaz), who said, "Why are you not completing your book? Focus on your writing ability and chase your dream of coming out with a book every year."

My colleagues at ZTE provided me with enough space to put down my thoughts. They contributed lots of perspectives to lead me to write something interesting. I would like to thank my friends and colleagues from China for encouraging me with their critical feedback on my articles.

My close friends Vikas and Jyoti Kumar and Priti Singh were always there sharing their thought-provoking ideas. They ignited new concepts in my mind. I would humbly take the opportunity to thank my senior colleagues for mentoring and guiding me. They have been patiently taking out time to read my published articles and providing their inputs. I am genuinely indebted to them.

A very special thank to Mr. A.P. Parigi Sir for going through the manuscript several times and sharing his feedbacks. He strengthened my belief that it can come out better.

And, of course, my lovely Sharan family, who have been there through thick and thin and encouraged me to write, write and write and continued their faith in me.

I could not have finished it without the support from my son Sarthak, who curbed his itching for *"ghoomne chalo"* on weekends and sacrificed his holidays to let me complete this manuscript. My pet dog Steif, who sat through my writing sessions quietly beside me, was another big motivator.

And I must thank the Notion Press team for being patient with me and supporting me in every step of publishing etc. Big thanx to you for making my dream come true.

I am sure I am missing out many who directly or indirectly influenced me positively. A BIG thank you to them. Thank you, all. I am indebted.

1

Touch Matters

A few years back, I had attended two interviews with two different organisations from the same industry. I generally prefer early morning flights to reach the venue on time. Both the interviews were with very large organisations and were for mid-level positions. Interestingly, these two experiences have very long-lasting impacts.

Retro-1

I was on my way to the Delhi Airport to catch a 5 a.m. flight for Mumbai. It was 4 in the morning, and I calculated that I would comfortably reach by 4.15 a.m. at the Delhi Airport. Around 7.50, from Mumbai Airport, I took a cab to reach the venue in the city. Since it was a little early for work, around 8.45, I was at the office and was greeted by the security guard and was offered a seat. While waiting at the reception, I thanked my decision of taking an early morning flight, as I was there before 9 a.m., comfortably before office timings. Around 9.10, the receptionist arrived, and after enquiring about the purpose, she was courteous enough to offer tea. Undoubtedly, after the early morning flight, the tea tasted like *amrit* (nectar). By the time I finished my tea it was 9.35, and I could see a few people arriving for work. It was a normal working day, and employees had started arriving, so I requested the receptionist to seat me in some meeting room or conference room to avoid encountering known faces. This is one of the flipsides of working in the same industry for long. There is always a huge possibility of crossing somebody known at the wrong time, and then being bombed with a volley of questions like, *"Arey app yahan?"*, *"Yahan kaise?"*, *"Kisse milna hai?"*, *"Acha wo abhi bhi wahin hain ya unhone change kar liya job.*" (Hey, how come you are here? Whom are you meeting? Ooh, x person is still there? I was assuming that he might have changed jobs by now.)

Though most of them do not have any evil intent for doing this, surely one would get embarrassed to be caught at the wrong time in the wrong place. It becomes more hilariously embarrassing when one tries giving lame excuses knowing very well that the other person knows well that he is there for the interview, both playing dumb with each other! During my career, I have encountered some funny incidents being on the other side of the table. One of the most comedic situations was when one of my team members accidently invited two people from the same department from the same organisation for an interview on the same day. The recruiter was newly hired from the FMCG industry and was just two weeks old in the organisation. She was assigned the profile of hiring senior and mid-level customer service positions. By mistake, she invited both of them on the same day unknowingly. The usage of different registered licence names of their organisation by both the candidates as their current organisation led to the confusion. Both of them were invited from Bangalore, and the timings for the interviews were first half and second half. Once the error was found out, the HR Team had to use the best of their wit and jugglery to manage the interviews so that both did not come face to face with each other. Moreover, the relationship between the candidates was of member and manager. The Recruitment Manager shared the situation with the interview panel and suggested that they take the interviews discreetly on different floors of the building. First, the interview of the manager was concluded and then the interview of the team member was taken. While the interview of the team member was ongoing, the senior one was ushered into the CEO's room for the final interview. With great support from the panel members, along with the CEO and the receptionist, the interviews were conducted smoothly, and both did not cross each other. The sensitivity and sanctity of their identities were maintained.

Here, in my case, I got a feeling after interacting with the receptionist that the organisation was on a recruitment spree and they were conducting regular "interviews." Hence, it was a routine activity for the receptionist. At my request, she instantly checked and seated me in a cosy meeting room, which I presumed was vacant, as I was the first person to arrive at the venue.

But my trauma was yet to start! Till 11 a.m., I was in the same meeting room and had met up with the HR executive several times, who apologised saying that the concerned person was in a meeting and would meet soon. If I recollect correctly, the executive's body language was pretty robotic. The executive would come, apologise for the delay and go back, all in the span of three to four minutes. Finally, my wait ended, and I was ushered in for the first round of meeting at around 11.45. This went off pretty coolly, and post meeting, my interviewer suggested that I needed to meet the Business Head for the next round, so I was asked to wait for *some time.* I went back to the same meeting room to wait. Around 1 p.m., I was invited for lunch by the HR executive, though, unfortunately, he had no clue about when the next interview would happen.

The lunch experience was another interesting one. I had lunch alone though I was invited by the executive, but he excused himself on the pretext of some urgent meeting! Post lunch, I moved back to my meeting room. This time, I was less stressed and less conscious than I was in the morning, as I was tuned to the place around. By now, I was pretty comfortable with the room and was aware of all the furniture, paintings, size of the table, etc. It is human tendency to get acquainted first with the "materialistic items" around him/her faster. Around 4.30 p.m., my luck shined, and I was ushered into the Business Head's room and met him. He was a pass out from a premium management school and had been with the organisation for more than seven years. We spent around forty-five minutes. During the interview, one could easily guess that he was fully awed by the promoter's family and had dropped promoter names at least fifteen times during the discussion.

I could sense through the discussions that he was close to promoters and had some kind of "by-passing" reporting relationship also. Interestingly, during discussions on various situations, he shared his own experience of how his boss had handled them (please read here promoter, though on paper he was reporting to somebody else). He did not mince words in making it clear that "there is no closing time for work hours in his organisations, and people work passionately till late evenings, around 9ish or 10 p.m." I should correct myself for using the word "sense," rather he made me feel it in words. In some organisations in India, especially where promoters/owners are involved, there is always a chunk of people who have some kind of access to them irrespective of where they fall in the organisational structure. After the interaction was over, we shook hands, and I left the room. He dropped me up to the door of his cabin. I waited for around fifteen minutes for the executive, assuming he would come over, but then I messaged him finally saying that I was through with both meetings and if there was nothing more planned then I would prefer to rush to the airport, as my flight back was at 8 p.m. The executive came and thanked me, and we parted. Before leaving, I was asked for the ticket details and expenses, and I was assured that the reimbursement would be sent in the next two weeks.

Retro-2

It was 8 p.m., and the next day I had to appear for an interview. *Beep. Beep.* I received a message on my phone. It read: "*Good evening, Mr. Sharat. This is Mukesh, Admin Manager. Driver's number has been messaged to you. He will pick you up from the airport. Wish you a safe journey. In case you need any help pl. feel free to call me.*" WOW. It was so sweet of them. Never expected them to do this; at least I had not expected this kind of gesture, as interviews are part and parcel of an employee's life. I took the morning flight as per schedule and reached there. The moment I landed in the city of Ahmedabad and switched on my phone after landing, I found a missed call from the driver. He had arrived around fifteen minutes back and was waiting for me to come out of the airport. I got into the vehicle. It was a neat one, and the driver drove me to a hotel near the office and said, "Sir, *aap yahan fresh ho lein* (Sir, you take rest here and freshen up)." I was surprised and rather taken aback. I had already freshened up at the airport and was not prepared for this. I was not very keen on staying in a hotel, as it would be an unexpected, wasteful expense. But with no option, I went inside the hotel and shared my information with the receptionist. It was a four star hotel. The receptionist allotted me a nice room. I was thinking about the billing like any normal human being. I think the receptionist could gauge this or maybe she was trained in handling the guests because she said, "Sir, the breakfast and room charges are to be borne by the organisation. You please share your visiting card." I smiled and thanked her for her courtesy. Of course, it was a big relief, but I didn't show it on my face. But she insisted on informing that it was a corporate tie up! Great.

By the time I moved towards the elevator, I got a call from the Admin Manager, "Good morning. Hope you are comfortable. If you need anything, please ask the reception. Since the interviews will be at 10.30, we will pick you up at 10.00, as the office is next door. You can have a short nap and get fresh. We will meet at the office." Very sweet, courteous and considerate! This was just very different from many of my earlier experiences. I should confess that I myself do not offer such courtesy in my organisation.

Around 10 a.m., I went out after having a light breakfast. I opted for fruits with a little *poha* (local dish) and masala tea. I chose to walk down to the office, as it was just a few hundred metres away. At the office reception, I shared my name with the receptionist and informed that I was there to meet the Chief HR Officer for an interview. She ushered me into a meeting room at the end of the lobby. It was a small but tidy meeting room with a side table, two chairs and a small book shelf. Of course, not to miss was a map on the wall mentioning the areas where they have businesses. The office boy came with tea within ten minutes, followed by a senior HR member and the Admin Manager, who dropped in to say hello. Both spent around twenty minutes talking casually about the city, the people and traffic.

At 10.25, I was invited for the interview with the Chief HR Officer (CHRO). The CHRO was very polite and humble in his interactions. He initiated the discussion by sharing about his experience in the organisation and how much he liked the city. He was from East India and studied in Delhi. We interacted, and he shared the expectations of the job and about the organisation. The gentleman spent a good amount of time discussing the role, structure and culture and how they had built this organisation. One could sense his connect and sense of belongingness to the organisation during the discussion. He was driven by a sense of ownership and did not reflect an iota of arrogance in it.

Post meeting, I was back to the room, and soon the senior HR person who I had met in the morning came down. We talked about the organisation's culture and business challenges for another half an hour, and later, he suggested that we have an early lunch in the café on the rooftop so that we could talk more. During the conversation, I could sense it was more of an informal interview, but yes, in a more comfortable way.

Soon after lunch, I met the Business Head. He was an IIT + IIM (Indian Institute of Technology + Indian Institute of Management – two premium technical and management institutes of global standard) combo who was with the organisation for the last 6 years and had moved to Ahmedabad from Bangalore. The moment I settled in his office, he opened with the statement, "What would you like to have? Tea or coffee? Our filter coffee is very nice; you must try it." It was one of the best possible ways to put strangers at ease. In fact, I believe that pleasantries with informal discussion not only help the candidate in settling down faster but also end up having more meaningful discussion. In fact, he initiated a discussion about how he and his family were settled and how the organisation and his team helped him and a few others coming from the south to settle. By now I was totally at ease. During the interaction, the subject revolved around seeking my views and opinions on certain situations like motivation for new employees to join from other cities or how to address a good performer who suddenly got derailed and was not performing for the last two-three months. Another interesting situation discussed was about a manager who insisted on promoting a star performer out of the promotion cycle and was strongly battling for it. On serious note, he shared that the role of Business Head becomes more challenging, handling internal pressures from managers.

Post meeting, the admin guy along with the Senior HR person dropped me to the car that was to take me to the airport. Just before parting, he suggested that I pick up some *dhoklas* (local snack), which are popular, on the way. They suggested the shop from where to pick it up to the driver. Let me not forget to add here that my ticket was pre-booked by the organisation already.

Both the experiences were from the same kind of industry with two large groups of India. Both are very large organisations with national presence. Both have their own "Sensitivity" quotient. For one, it was more of a professional interaction – "Business to Business," while for the other it was more about "Responsibility and taking Pride in People." This may be ONE odd case for them, but for a candidate like me, it was an impactful EXPERIENCE that left a long-lasting impression. One is driven by mechanised ROBOTIC culture, while the other is influenced by sensitivity culture. It is a clear reflection of their cultures. In both the situations, one could see that the whole ecosystem from top to bottom displayed the same culture. The behaviour of the top man can be felt even at the level of reception. EVERYONE BEHAVES AND DISPLAYS THE SAME CULTURE. From Administration to the Hotel to the CEO, all displayed the same culture.

If we do a drill down of these two incidents, then a few interesting observations will come out.

The leader is observed: The behaviour of the leader is observed very minutely by the organisation. All employees in the organisation start behaving in the same way that the leader behaves. A few follow it assuming it to be the organisation's culture, while others do it for appeasement. But the bottom line is that most follow it!

Like in the first organisation, making candidates wait for long and not being concerned about her/his privacy reflects their "insensitive and callous" attitude. It reflects the organisation's mindset that it is an "EMPLOYER MARKET" and not an "EMPLOYEE MARKET," and hence, employees will always be valued less. Further, the interaction with the Business Head reflects its "arrogance." In the second organisation, however, the whole experience can be dubbed as a "brand-building effort."

It was very evident in both the cases that the teams down the line were *fully aware of the way the candidate would be treated by the Business Head;* hence, their behaviour with the candidate was a "replica" of the same. In one case, it was "Come and Go," while in the other case, the intent was "Can we make it better?"

To put a pause to this storytelling, I would like to add an interesting fact: The first organisation had a larger employee base (more than double the number of the second organisation), but its revenue and EBIDTA was lower than the second one. The per employee revenue ratio was approx. 3:1. Can we sum it up with a simple question: Is this result due to the culture?

2

Is It CSR or a Branding Opportunity @ My Lala Company!!!!

These days, the Indian media is flooded with news of impactful contribution by business and social leaders like Mr. Azim Premji, Ratan Tata, Narayan Murthy, Nandan Nilekani and many others giving back to the society in a big way. They are the new influencers of the society, motivating to do good. They are the new "change leaders" who are seriously contributing towards making the world a better place to live in. They, along with many others, have changed the real meaning of CSR (Corporate Social Responsibility) in our country. They have already made a place for themselves by building great corporations, and now they are back in the news again for different but better reasons. They are setting a new road map for the society, and their acts are being followed positively by the media that has christened them as "New HOPE!" Media and communication channels are abuzz with them, talking about them for a right cause. Our government has also played a positive role in building the culture of social responsibility along with laying down laws for it. The law on CSR has its own positive impact in social development areas.

Amidst this positive environment, one should not be surprised to find some smarties taking advantage of it with their own interpretations of CSR like the one shared below. One of the domestic promoter-driven organisations that was interested in the manufacturing business also decided to set up a CSR Department after the law was enacted. It was a mid-level organisation that grew from a small medicine factory to an organisation with five manufacturing plants. Its headquarter was located in Pune with plants around the states of Maharashtra, Tamil Nadu and Orissa.

Their journey had been good, and in ten years, their annual turnover had grown to the tune of four thousand crore rupees. In their pursuit to grow, they had recently hired a few senior and mid-level professionals from reputed MNC organisations to strengthen their business. The professionals were inducted with a fair amount of empowerment.

To strengthen this organisational structure, a board was constituted to oversee the business performance with enough empowerment to the professional leaders to run the business. But, on the other hand, family members were also a part of the organisation with an unwritten free hand in operations, like any other promoter-driven lala organisation. A few of the senior ones handling the different departments were the uncles and brothers.

The organisation was led by a young first-time entrepreneur-promoter who had started this business without any particular previous experience. He was a sincere and people-centric person with an ambition to grow. Considering the modest beginning of the organisation, the success was commendable. The organisation had some good and innovative HR practices, and one of them was partially providing scholarship assistance with college fees to the children of employees. They also had the provision for providing "interest-free soft loans" for house or marriage purposes. It was usually given to loyal employees who had been with them since ages. The loan was provided interest free with a long-term repayment plan, which could be as long as 5 years or so. These were innovative and sensitive efforts made by the promoter to drive loyalty amongst the employees, by touching their lives.

Due to business reasons and a desire to grow faster, they had taken high loans from banks and hence were burdened with serious debt from banks as well as vendors. The financial culture was driven by an unwritten management principle of *"pay timely interest, procure more loans and recycle it to pay interest."* Interest payment delay was seen as a serious noncompliance by the management and was never encouraged. They were very sensitive about their image of "non-defaulting organisation" and never wanted to jeopardise it to impact their future loan opportunities.

Some interesting behaviour patterns could be seen flowing from the top such as:

1. Continuous procurement of loans: "Keep taking loans. But never default in interest payment." Their banking team within the finance department was a large one. Their core KPI was to maintain a good level of engagement with all the banks. The senior ones were expected to engage with higher ups, while the other members of the teams were responsible for engaging and managing relationships with the rest of the levels at the bank. Efforts were on to keep every level of banks engaged in some way or the other in a structured way.

2. The next unwritten rule was in Vendor Management: There was delayed payment to vendors; the ideal time to review and process bills of vendors was around 6 months, with final pay out of 80% maximum! The whole financial system worked around these philosophies and thought processes.

3. Played it safe. Engaged with Public Sector banks only: They believed that Public Sector banks were safer and easier to manage in spite of their bureaucratic processes. They had a belief that these banks were less ruthless in recovery and more understanding. They never engaged with any MNC or local private bank.

With the government regulation of law enactment on CSR for organisations, they also came up with a CSR Department and hired the CSR team from the industry. They hired a professional named Mannu Chabra from the industry who was number 2 in a very large organisation. As per the CSR roll out strategy, they decided to work on healthcare. The plan was made to provide medical assistance to workers living near plants. To support it, 5 ambulances were procured, one ambulance for each plant. It was a decent start off. The ambulances were inaugurated with great pomp and show by the CM and the Industry and Finance Ministers of the state.

In one of the department meetings of CSR, it was proposed to expand the healthcare services to villages near the plant. The villages identified were in the vicinity of a 10 km radius, and many workers came from these villages. Due to a lack of proper medical facilities in these villages, frequent absenteeism was a major concern due to self or family illness.

Mannu prepared a detailed proposal for procuring one additional ambulance with the latest equipment fitted in to function as a "mobile dispensary-cum-rescue system." The proposal was prepared keeping a 2-year operating budget and was submitted to the CFO for approval. It was decided to deploy it in the nearby villages around their largest plant in Orissa. When the paper was submitted for approval to the CFO, who was the brother of the Promoter, he insisted that it should be publicised and projected as "CSR for 5."

"Let's brand it properly in the media and social circle. It should look like a game-changing social initiative by the organisation. *Isko aisa prastut kariye taki ye lagey ki hum eek nahin panch plant mein start karney waaley hain. Aur ye sahi bhi hai hum future main paanch mein ambulance dalenge!*" He wanted this effort to be projected by the media and social circle in such a way that it seemed like the organisation had invested in a big way in all ambulances and the Chairman had adopted those villages! *Kshetra ki swasthya sudhar pragati mein ye eek anootha yogdaan rahega bhaiya ji ka* (It will look like a big contribution to the development of health care)."

LO. Are you surprised? No, I think, other than Mannu, no one in the room was surprised or amused by this suggestion. And the amusement was clearly visible on Mannu's face, trying to understand the objective of it. The proposal was communicated in a very casual way and was accepted. All other members present there echoed in one single voice, categorising it as a "great idea." It was an acceptable norm for them – invest in 1, showcase more. The interesting part was the intent & mindset behind this thought. CSR was seen as an INVESTMENT with the expectation of RETURN. After all, they were doing CHARITY; hence, Branding became their RIGHT!

Hold on; there were more surprises to come during the period between conceptualisation and inauguration. Mannu was an experienced and respected professional from a private banking industry. He tried to control his reactions and got into the preparation. It was decided that the inauguration of medical services would take place on the birthday of the promoter's grandfather. Yes, nothing could be more auspicious than this day! Mannu chose not to comment on it and carried on with the preparation, as there were just 12 days left to make this event successful.

The preparation was in full swing. The purchase order was issued to the ambulance manufacturing company in Pune on the 3rd day as per the specifications procured from top hospitals. The ambulance was to be equipped with all the comfort and emergency equipment to ferry far-flung patients to nearby hospitals. The ambulance was equipped for serious heart patients and accident victims also. It was a state-of-the-art ambulance.

Meanwhile, the CFO thought of checking with their family doctor to confirm if it was in line with the requirement. The family doctor was the director of a highly reputed south Mumbai hospital. The CFO asked his secretary to send the details through email along with photographs of the ambulance to the doctor. **To his surprise, the response came from the doctor the very next day, and it was something which changed the whole event.** The doctor remarked that this ambulance design was comparable with any western country's ambulance. It was fitted with high-quality equipment. He congratulated the CFO for such a unique thought. He further added a cherry on it by stating that there were very few such ambulances in our country and it was probably the first in the state where they were putting it.

The CFO could not hold himself and immediately called Mannu and congratulated him for such a good design saying, *"Bahut badhiya opinion aaya hai ambulance ki. Aapko to pata hi hai ki main kitni seriously sey kaam karta hoon. Aakhir company ka maamla hai aur mera jivan iss company ke liye hai. Koi aisa kaam nahi honey doonga jo apni company ke liye nuksaan dayak ho. Maine Dr. Motwani se feedback liya tha. Unka bahut badhiya report aaya hai. Wo bahut prasann hain. Kehtey hain aapki company barabar achaa kaam karti hai* (Very positive opinion has come from Doctor Motwani. You know very well how serious I am about the company. I do not do anything which can harm the organisation's image. Doctor Motwani is very happy and has commented that our organisation always does great work)." He further added, *"Aapko badhiya bonus doonga Mannu ji, maan khush kar diya hai aapne. Mera sujhaw hai aap mukhyamantri ji aur health minister ji ko bhi bulayen inauguration mein. Main yahan se chairman, unki maata ji pitaji aur unki pariwar ke anya sadasyon ko bhi bolta hoon wahan pahunchen. Aur haan aap media ka bandobast acha karen. Chinta mat kariye baki arrangement main dekh loonga* (I will give you very good bonus. You have made my soul happy. My suggestion is to invite the Chief Minister of the state along with Health Minister for inauguration. I will invite our honourable Chairman and his family along with his parents and request their presence there on inauguration day. And yes please make very good arrangements for media. Don't worry about anything. I will support you with all the resources)." It was a god-sent opportunity for branding in the press, media, social and political circle, and the CFO was just not ready to lose it.

The inauguration day started with hectic activity. The time of inauguration was planned for 10.30 a.m. when the Chief Minister would arrive. Mannu and team reached the venue at 7 a.m. to oversee the arrangement. He was not surprised to find the CFO also reaching there around 7.30! After all, it was the matter of his *izzat* (pride). The team counterchecked with the media and other invitees to reconfirm their availability. They were relieved to know that they were all attending.

The family of the promoter had already reached the city the previous night through an Air India flight. The family was staying with the CFO whereas other senior members from the Head Office checked in at a 5 star hotel. The bookings were made already in advance. By 9 a.m., family members arrived at the venue dressed in traditional clothes. They were joined by the family and friends of the CFO. By 10 a.m., most of the other dignitaries and the Minister of Health and Minister of Heavy Industries arrived there, and they all waited for the CM. In between, 30 times, the CFO went to Mannu to reconfirm, "*Saab control mein hai naa* (Hope everything is under control)?"

Mannu knew very well that the focus should be more on the media and press management, as the CFO and the organisation would be keener to know "how much it was talked about." He decided to engage the promoter's wife to hand over gifts to the media guests for a more personalised touch. He suggested it to the CFO, and he willingly invited the promoter's wife and his mother to do the honours. "*Sahi salaah hai ye. Bilkul appnapan mehsoos karenge mehman. Aakhir atithi hain wo hamare* (Very good suggestion. Media invitees will feel personal touch. After all, they are our guests here)." The gifts were meticulously chosen by him two days earlier. He ensured that everybody got the same quality of gift so that undue negativity could be avoided. Equal treatment was given to both smaller media brands and reputed brands of the media. The goody bag consisted of leaflets about the organisation, its CSR initiatives, write up of press releases consisting of comments from the promoter, CFO and the Managing Director along with bottles of good quality imported liquor and a voucher worth Rs. 2100 from a big retail showroom.

The inauguration went off smoothly on the auspicious day of the late grandfather's birthday. The CM inaugurated it with a long speech, dedicating it to the state. He was accompanied by the Health Minister, local MPs and local MLAs. Prominent news channels and newspapers covered the event. They took bytes and interviews of the

Chief Minister, other ministers and the promoter. Mannu ensured that this coverage would be in some or the other media for the next three to four days by arranging invites to senior members from the headquarter to join talk shows at the local level. They joined the discussion forums on TV and radio channels talking about the initiative. He knew very well that in the corporate world, he needed to keep the other "power centres of the headquarter" also happy, as they had "nuisance value." Only keeping the promoter and family happy would not be helpful in the **long run.**

Interesting Impacts

Prominent news coverage came in all local newspapers and local and national TV channels, which talked about the great effort towards social health and the company's plan of donating 5 ambulances. Some described the organisation as a "Social Champion of the State." Others carried the news as *"Swasthya Samadhan* (health solution)." Local channels spoke very highly about the efforts and carried technical details about the ambulance and its utilisation. A few even went a step ahead and carried opinions from renowned doctors of the region talking about how these could bring a change in "Emergency Services" and how others should follow the same in the interest of the state.

Needless to say, Mannu and his team were rewarded with lucrative bonuses. The total cost incurred on travel of family members and senior employees, inauguration arrangement, gifts to local leaders, press, media and distinguished guests and donation to party fund was phenomenally high compared to the cost of the ambulances. In monetary terms, the company splashed more money on the CSR branding than on the ambulance.

At times, while introspecting, Mannu felt that the cost of branding was not only limited to the opportunity lost in procuring one more ambulance, but also, in the long run, it was an opportunity lost for those who needed treatment in remote locations around the plants but could not get it due to the non-availability of proper medical care. Wouldn't it be good if organisations start thinking of devising a mechanism where "the impact of CSR efforts are evaluated through other modes in line with Gallup or Aon satisfaction surveys from the beneficiary community?"

3

Performance Management or Relationship Management?

I t's the noon of 27ᵗʰ of September. Unlike other months, this 27ᵗʰ is different and more important, as the Human Resource Department (HRD) has to submit the payroll details to the finance department for the auditing and processing of salary. This month, the management has also decided to release the annual performance bonus for the last calendar year, thus making this payroll more critical. Yes, we are right in interpreting that the calendar year means January to December and performance pay-outs being made in September is too late. Ideally, most of the organisations with this financial year cycle (April to March cycle) release their performance bonus by May or June.

The Payroll Manager Salman Shaikh is stuck and is struggling to get the final approval from the management to submit it to finance. The back-ending is already done, and the list needs to reach finance before 3 p.m. to enable the salary along with bonus to be credited to the employees' bank account by 30ᵗʰ September.

He looks for a message in his mobile again to check if there is any response from the HR Head. It is the umpteenth time he has checked and has been continuously checking every 5 minutes!! He gets up and starts walking to the office of the HR Head and reminds him, "Boss, please remind the CEO about the approval. It is getting late. We might fail the deadline. It has been pending with him for more than four days. I think we should go to his office to request him to approve it." But oh! Looking at the reaction of his boss, he feels as if he has made a very weird proposal to him. The expression on the HR Head's face is enough to reflect his "frustration topped with helplessness." Mohit, the HR Head, is an old timer in the organisation and has seen the organisation from very close. He knows the DNA of the organisation very well. It is an organisation with autocratic and cadre-driven culture, where processes are dependent on the person sitting at the top. Meeting the CEO for small issues is just not appreciated, and bonuses to employees are not looked at as important issues. Yes, you heard it right – employee issues are not seen as an important factor. So, both Salman and his boss Mohit have to wait, and they continue to wait.

The story is not over. Surprises are yet to unfold here.

Around 2.30 p.m., Mohit comes jumping to Salman saying, "I have got the approval from the CEO. Please process it." He sounds excited like as if he has climbed Mount Everest. Salman moves to his laptop to check the approval and send the file to the finance department. Just before he is about to send the file, he is stopped by his boss Mohit, who interrupts softly, "Hey, there are a few changes suggested. We can process it after making these small changes." The message is communicated very softly to Salman with a touch of regret.

The pay-out proposal was prepared based on a formula, and every employee was being paid as per the formula. They had designed the policy and had taken every stakeholder through it in one-on-one meetings. The final policy design was prepared capturing inputs provided by a few of them. Mohit had presented this policy after taking inputs from all to the committee and getting it approved by them. Moreover, the policy was approved by the CEO also. The objective of this exercise was to standardise the process and bring transparency into the system. The HR department firmly believes that standard process and formula-based calculations also help in easy understanding and acceptability by employees. Hence, any change at this juncture is a big surprise to Salman and his team.

He gets the shock of his life when he looks at the "small changes" suggested by the CEO. The so-called "small changes" are 10 in number, and all 10 are senior employees from the total base of 200 eligible employees. Interestingly, 8 of them are to be given a higher bonus than the recommendation based on policy and the other 2 are to be given a bonus lower than the recommendation based on the formulae. And the catch is – all changes are to be made without increasing the overall budget! It is not an easy task to make changes maintaining the same cost. He has to change the whole formulae. In order to make these 8 "happy," he has to reduce the bonuses of the remaining 190 employees. That's the power of "CEO approval." The Payroll Manager is mature enough to resist his temptation of pushing his HR Head to discuss with the CEO again. He pities the poor HR Head and leaves the idea of discussion knowing very well that when reminding the CEO for approval is such a big fuss, then no way is his boss going to discuss it again with the CEO for reconsideration.

Who are these 10 cases? Those 2 victimised cases were incidentally rated well in their PMS (Performance Management System) evaluation by their supervisor, but at the time of giving bonus these two were being "penalised" by the management. Later, in an informal gathering, the Payroll Manager is informed about these 10 cases. They are the examples of the so-called "Recency Syndrome." The bonus was calculated on the last CALENDER year performance (January to December performance), but in the last one month (actually in the last three weeks), these 8 cases have been able to impress upon the CEO about their potential value addition while the other two failed.

After two drinks and hearing out the story, Salman feels like he is living in a "feudalistic culture" where the appeasement and happiness of the feudal lord overrules all processes and policies. The powerful Lord needs to be kept in good humour always for rewards. It matters the most how your chips are rated on the particular day of decision. It is more shocking to know that the Performance Measurement System rating has in no way any link to any kind of reward or bonus. And he was laughing when it was shared that "the star employee awardee of this year was actually evaluated average in the last two quarterly reviews."

From the management perspective, it is common practice to get these kinds of changes. Salman knew very well that at times business reasons compel the changes and it is right for the management to have the last say on these rewards. After all, the management is responsible for the overall business success, and their judgement should be respected. They do understand the business repercussions, and it is expected that any decision they take is based on a long-term perspective based on ethics and processes. He had experienced such incidents which are commonly known as "management quota or discretion" in previous organisations as well. The earlier organisations' management also had been tweaking the rewards and bonuses pay-outs, but it was backed with "reasoning and logic."

He clearly remembered how one of his previous Managing Directors wanted to give additional bonus to one of the R&D employees, but was not very comfortable doing it blatantly. He wanted to do it in a more acceptable way. To seek guidance, he invited Salman and his Head of HR to seek their views. His Head of HR was a very sharp and balanced person, and Salman always admired him. He suggested introducing a category of "Special allowance for top performers from each Business Unit." The suggestion was wholeheartedly supported by the Managing Director. As a result, this new special allowance was extended to four more employees from four different business units. Though it was a small increase in the overall budget, with this initiative they could maintain the sanctity of the process. And further, with the introduction of the Special Allowance category, they were successful in preparing a competitive environment for others, and till date his earlier organisation is continuing to reward the best ones from business units, and now he had lately heard that this has become a part of the Annual Reward List also.

The difference between his old and current organisation lies in "intent and attitude." The previous management, while making "such changes," was clear about not hurting their image internally and externally. They took care of their image. They were very conscious about the impact on people and never wanted to demotivate their own people. Hence they chose the simple process of "doing the wrong in the right way!"

4

Recruiting the Right Match or Ego Match?

"**I** really need to get these Project Managers on boarded ASAP, without any delay, or else we might lose the future business," Amulya commented exasperatedly to his manager Kartik after coming out from a customer review meeting. This was the third weekly review which went bad due to a delay in release. It was a new VFX project from a very new customer from the Netherlands.

Amulya had been trying to do his best to put the delivery in order but was not able to meet the customer's requirement. He had been with the organisation for the last 4 years and had handled several projects effectively. It was not that he had not faced challenges earlier, but somehow he had always been able to streamline the project delivery within two weeks. Unfortunately, in this project, he had not been able to manage it, and he was not blaming the customer, as he knew very well that they were also under pressure. The service-level agreement (SLA) was tight, rather very tight. The organisation knew from day one that the SLA's expectations were high, and the customer had made it very clear during the negotiation about it. In fact, the customer had allowed them to bill 10% additional manpower cost into the proposal knowing the pressure.

It was a fault from his organisation's side, as they had taken it lightly hoping that the same set of existing employees would be able to manage the additional work pressure. But, unfortunately, it was not happening. While they could meet the number deadline, when it came to quality, they were getting 22% flaws in output. In the last three weeks, the quality score was 22% lesser than the agreed SLA due to various reasons. Amulya had realised that there was an immediate need for an efficient Project Manager who could ensure that proper steps and processes were followed. The flaws were due to missing out on defined steps. While reviewing it internally, he observed that while correcting the old flaws, at times, teams were making new mistakes. It was a clear lack of **structured work.**

"This is becoming a serious issue, Kartik. Neither the numbers are meeting nor is there any improvement in quality score. Unfortunately, in the last three weeks, your team has not been able to even identify the crux of the problem. Please take it seriously, as we are running out of time, and please do not make us believe that our decision of partnering with you was a mistake," Malcom, the production director from the customer's side, had remarked today. The customer was losing patience.

Amulya sent a mail to the HR department to recruit three Project Managers ASAP. The Recruitment Manager Manish was an old timer in the organisation and had grown from ranks. He forwarded the requirement to his colleague Sandhya to identify and shortlist candidates for the final interview. Sandhya got into the job and started referring to her data bank. She had given herself 3 working days to find the right candidates. She had internally kept the target of 6 shortlisted candidates for these two positions. Manish was confident in her capability and was assured that she would fill these positions soon. She had joined his team a year back and had handled a couple of critical positions. Since she had joined from a different industry, in the initial few months, she was not assigned sensitive positions. She was the replacement for an earlier person who had left abruptly without giving any notice due to her husband's transfer to Hong Kong and had left with open vacancies. Within 2 months, Sandhya got a grip over the pending work and got all the vacant positions filled.

Five days after the last incident, Kartik walked down to the Recruitment Manager Manish's office and shared a profile with him.

"We have selected these two candidates for the position; please issue them the offer letters. They are available for immediate joining."

"Thanks, Kartik, I will arrange the interview with them and will decide based on merit," responded Manish.

"No, no, please make offers to them immediately. Boss has recommended it," he insisted. His discomfort was visible at the delay of the offer. "We are under tremendous pressure and cannot afford any more delay. I hope you will understand," said Kartik.

"Sandhya has already lined up 3 more candidates this week. What about the other candidate you met this Monday? What's his feedback? He is good and has excellent reference from the Market," suggested Manish. "No, he is rejected. Not good for Project Manager," Kartik replied curtly.

Manish was zapped, as he knew well that the candidate was good and would add lots of value to the organisation. Everyone had liked him. Moreover, he was selected by this gentleman Kartik also. Now what had prompted him to drop this candidate and push the other candidate for the offer? He was curious to know the real reason behind this U turn. So, he decided to dig deeper into it. To his astonishment, Manish found that the candidate was dropped not due to competence but was dropped due to "new referred candidates." He knew how to get to the root of this mega U turn. He knew Kartik very well and respected him for his integrity and seriousness. It was hard to believe that Kartik was pushing these cases. There must be some other pressure points.

So he kept quiet, and in the evening he walked up to Kartik and asked him if he would like to join him for masala chai (spice-flavoured tea). He knew very well that Kartik was fond of masala chai from the tea stall vendor across the street. The tea stall across the street was the "multipurpose spot" for employees from most of the nearby organisations. Employees used to go there for smoking and stress busting. Any time of the day, one could find 10 to 15 employees from nearby organisations there. It was a place where one could get loads of information and gossip. In fact, Manish at times had got good references from there by eavesdropping on the gossip of employees of other organisations. The last one, he remembered, was a mid-level manager, who had a showdown with his manager during appraisal and had come down to the tea stall in a frustrated mood with two other colleagues. During their discussion, Manish overheard the word "data analyst" and chose to stay there for some more time. Then he moved to them and asked them if they had a lighter to light his cigarette. One of them gave him the lighter from his pocket. He returned it, thanking him, and introduced himself to them and asked the data analyst to share his number. He later approached the candidate over the phone and invited him for the interview, and within two days, the offer was made to him. The person was not happy with his current organisation anyway and hence did not take more than two weeks to join.

Manish took Kartik down to the tea stall for masala tea and started talking casually about the latest movie he had watched on Netflix. The movie was good, and he recommended that Kartik watch it while travelling back home by cab. After some casual talk, Manish said, *"Yaar, Kartik, I am asking Sandhya to issue offer letters to those candidates referred by you. I can understand the pressure on you. Please tell me if you have committed to a particular amount of salary also, so that Sandhya, while talking to them, is on the same page."*

"No, I don't have any idea about the salary commitment. My boss should know about it. I have no clue." He sounded irritated. Looks like he did not like the candidates being addressed as "YOUR REFERENCE." Then he opened up and shared that his boss, who was the Account Head of this client, was under pressure, as they were not able to meet the SLA. Hence, he chose to look for candidates who were familiar with the customers and were in their good books as vendor, partner or ex-employees. The objective of the Account Head was that these so-called known faces would help in managing the client. These known faces were expected to ensure that the client did not escalate issues and took a liberal view of the organisation.

"Do you think it will work?" asked Manish. "No, definitely not. This is a short cut. These guys do not match our requirements fully, but the Account Head feels that by doing it, the client's issues will be resolved. Instead he should get deeper into the root cause and look for corrective measures." He further stressed, "The client is paid as per the digital screens prepared by us. And if the screen quality is not good, it gets rejected by their production department. The simple thing to understand is that blurred animated screens do not earn money. So the client cannot sell half-baked films in the market. Who will pay for poor-quality films? And I'm scared that by doing this we are moving towards messing up our lives. In reality, the problem will not be solved, and I doubt the client will tolerate this output even if it is presented by a person known to them. No organisation makes compromises with their bottom line. Relationship cannot excuse flaws," concluded Kartik. Manish felt sad for him.

He knew it was due to the short-cut working style employed by some immature managers who believed in "management by relationship instead of management by delivering rightly." And in the long run, the organisation suffered, as no mature organisation would prefer to partner with them.

Manish had two options left: 1) To accept it or 2) Escalate to his HR Head. He kept thinking over this incident, and the more he thought about it the more it strengthened his belief about it being illogical. In fact, he had experienced such incidents that involved weird reasons for rejection in the past as well. He remembered an incident that had occurred three weeks back. One of his colleagues had joined the organisation on behalf of PE (Private Equity) fund. This PE fund was an international organisation promoted by an Asian organisation. As a part of the deal, the CFO and Strategy Head were supposed to be nominated from their side. This colleague was also a member of the team. Though the CFO and Strategy Head were mature and experienced professionals with strong credibility, a few of their team members handling important profiles were comparatively junior and lacked broader vision.

This foreign national colleague had interviewed a very senior person to join the strategy team. The candidate was working as a Vertical Head with an IT consulting organisation. He was head hunted by Manish's team, and they convinced him about the content of the role. The candidate was initially reluctant to join, but after multiple meetings with Manish he agreed to give it a try. Post interview, the feedback given back to Manish was that the candidate was not suitable, as he lacked subject knowledge about strategy. Manish was shocked to hear the word "inadequate," as the candidate was leading the same vertical in his current organisation, which was three times larger in turnover. He wanted to get to the real cause of this rejection and decided to check with the candidate. He called up the candidate in the evening. "Hi, how was the meeting? How did it go? Did you get the answer to your queries?" Manish asked him. The candidate responded, "Manish, I am thankful to you for arranging this meeting. But, I am not sure whether it was good or not because the whole interview was around execution-level discussion and nothing strategic was discussed. I think the interviewer was not sure about the company's long-term vision. I think we should not carry on with further meetings because the expectations were not clear. Honestly, I feel the requirement sounded like a manager-level profile with 90% transactional work." Manish tried his best to explain it to him by hiding behind the "communication and interpretation gap" and ended the call. He got the answer for this rejection. The reason was simple: "The interviewer was too junior to assess the senior-level candidate and could not relate to his strategic thoughts."

This is a common challenge faced by many recruitment experts from organisations which focus more on providing internal growth to employees in order to be cost effective. Some organisations do not have an adequate competency-based growth programme. Organisations at times fall into the trap of promoting "incapable people who are not ready to handle higher roles." These individuals are promoted based on their previous performance but do not have adequate capability to handle the next-level roles. They lack the aptitude and skills of strategic acumen or industry knowledge or the ability to handle pressure and most importantly the ability to work with a diverse team and people.

The solution to this is simple but bold: "Reward liberally but recruit and promote judiciously and selectively." One wrong person leads to long-term leakage in the capability talent pool. Incapable managers can only build a low-capability team.

5

Am I a Business President or a President – Sales?

"And the award goes to Anuj Saxena, General Manager Sales, Hospitality account." The announcement was made by the Master of Ceremony (MC) during the Reward and Recognition programme in Hotel Leela. But the clapping was not very audible. The MC invited the Business Head of the Infrastructure Division to come over to the stage and hand over the award to Anuj. The sound of clapping was not very high, and it was not a roaring applause. This was the 17th award out of the 20 listed for the day. Out of 20 awards, 12 went to the sales department. The rest were distributed as team performance awards.

Chief HR Officer Komal Chaudhry was surprised to find most of the employees standing outside the event hall and hovering around the drinks counter while the reward ceremony was going on inside. She found it amusing to see their lack of interest in the rewards ceremony.

Komal had joined the organisation a year back and had moved from an e-commerce organisation based out of Bangalore. Her previous organisation was into service business with more than 4000 employees at different levels. The business was doing well and had competition from domestic as well as MNC PE (Private Equity) backed organisations. Employee retention was one of the core focus areas of management, and hence, they had a serious focus on engagement. Reward and Recognition was one of the most hyped and talked about programmes in the organisation with a high level of employee participation. The cross-functional organising team was even found involved and preparing for it weeks in advance. It used to be lots of fun and *masti* (enjoyment). Reward and Recognition night was always celebrated as a day dedicated "to the employees", "by the employees" and "for the employees". The Department Heads and Vertical Heads used to spend a lot of time evaluating and discussing the awards. Most importantly, it had to be a well-organised and structured programme.

But here it was different. She remembered the same kind of environment and participation in the last event, which was organised just 3 months post her joining this organisation. However, from the organisation perspective, she had observed that the Reward and Recognition was given due importance, and efforts were always made to make it grand and extravagant. From the budgeting perspective, there were no major challenges, and management was liberal in allocating a good amount of budget for it. To make it an involved and engaged programme event, it was clubbed with family day, and families were invited to make it memorable. The management was sincere to connect with the employees and family. Teams were encouraged to participate in talent shows, and employees used to spend a lot of quality time on planning it. The event was a platform for employees and their families to demonstrate their hidden talents like music, dance, singing, painting, etc.

In spite of all the genuine efforts made by the management, Komal had noticed that very few families participated in the event, and much lower participation was observed from Non-Sales and Marketing departments. It was confusing, as she was not able to identify and understand the reasons for such low participation. She felt that the employees had no respect for such a beautiful event and that they did not take it seriously. She found them to be disengaged with the organisation.

"I do not understand why we even organise such events when employees are not keen on it," she was confronted by her team member Rohit. Rohit was the Engagement Manager and had put in lots of energy to make this programme a success, but the participation in the last three events had frustrated him. To make things worse for him, comments from two senior colleagues a few minutes back had irritated him more. They commented, "Why do you call it Reward & Recognition night? You should call it Sales Reward Night instead because you do not have respect for other functions. Good that we did not bring our families. You HR people would have made us feel more humiliated in front of our families." **Rohit just moved away without replying and went to the garden behind the hotel for a smoke. He was not in a good mood. His thoughts were interrupted by a call from Komal. "Where are you, Rohit? Please come on back stage," she called.**

Komal was thinking about the whole incident and was equally hurt by the way Rohit was treated by the two senior colleagues. She wanted to confront them and speak to them, but something stopped her from doing so. She was a mature professional with a strong Organisation Development background. She had worked on culture areas in her previous organisation. Analytics-led Culture was her forte. She always worked on data points to address behaviour or culture issues. Two questions were bothering her thoughts, pushing her to analyse deeply: Q1) Why were the employees not very participative in the R&R? And, Q2) Was it the employees' fault?

The more she thought over it, the more she believed that there was something more to it. It was not an open and shut case, and it needed to be seen from a larger perspective before rushing to any conclusion about the lacklustre show. She felt it was very imperative to go for a "health study of the culture" and identify the root cause and take corrective action for the long-term benefit of the organisation's culture. The positive points were that both the organisation and employees were GENUINELY KEEN on having the R&R. Hence, the "missing link" to bridge the gap to bring both parties together needed to be addressed. And she knew where to start from!

The next morning, when Komal entered the office, she was very relieved and relaxed. She stepped into the office of the President to discuss the incident. She had already messaged him the previous night seeking an appointment. The President was a young guy with sound experience of working in the industry. He was mature and reasonable and was considered to be a fair leader. Professionally, she found him grounded and logical and respected him for his sincerity. Her journey till now had been good with him. He had to his credit a few success stories, which made him more confident. Komal decided not to initiate the discussion on the subject herself. Instead, she wanted to lead the discussion in such a way that the President himself touched upon the R&R event.

She started the discussion around the process of handing over awards to those awardees who could not attend the programme due to some reasons. She suggested handing over these awards through senior team members who were travelling to the locations to hand it over to them.

He immediately agreed to the suggestion, and then he touched the subject of feedback on the programme. "How did the programme go? Hope people enjoyed," he asked. Komal was just waiting for the question. "It was a good programme, especially the business part where the organisation history and plan were discussed in a simplified way for the employees as well as their families. Families could connect with it better, and many felt comfortable about the organisation's future being bright. It was a big image-boosting exercise for all," she replied.

The President responded, "Yes, but I did not find many families; in fact, most were the same faces who had come last time also. Do you think the invites were sent properly? Why were all the families not there? Next time, we need to plan better." "But I must appreciate the work done by the team. They had done a good job. I suggest you take them out for dinner for their commendable work," the President suggested looking at her. He sounded genuine, and Komal felt that it was the right opportunity to pursue the discussion further. She replied, "Yes, the invites were sent properly; in fact, personal informal invites were also given. Moreover, 90% of the sales team was there in the programme. So, I do not think this could be the reason. The lower footfall was from non-sales teams, which, though larger in number, did not turn up."

"Hmm, yes, I think you are right. So, have you tried speaking to them about why they could not make it? It is an important event for employees and their families." He sounded concerned and was definitely not happy with the low interest in the event. She could sense his discomfort. She had seen the efforts of the President in turning around the organisation. He had sincerely worked over it and had led the organisation effectively, but in spite of his effort, he was not seen and looked up to as a "neutral leader!"

"If I am allowed to share my observation as a professional, can I share something?" Komal asked. "Yes, please. I would like your honest observation on it. You are the HR Head of the organisation, and in terms of people issues, you are a champion, and you should speak your mind," the President responded, encouraging her.

"The last few events have been worth observing. As an outsider, I have observed that there is a difference in the engagement level of Sales and Non-Sales employees," Komal shared. "70% of rewards go to sales people, while 30% is divided amongst the rest, which incidentally comprises 85% of our total employee base. With less recognition to them, it might be making them feel as if they are non-contributors to the organisation." She continued, "Did you notice that by the 10th award the clapping sound was mostly coming from one corner of the hall, and not the whole hall? And that side was mostly occupied by the Sales team. Do the Non-Sales teams think they are not a part of the programme? Or, rather, do they think this programme is for the Sales team only?" While elaborating her points, she was also looking keenly at the President to read his expressions and reactions. And on finding his reaction to be concerned, she continued, "I have got some feelers that most non-awardees and Non-Sales guys intentionally do not bring their families, as they do not want to feel humiliated in front of them." Komal softened her tone and stressed on the next line,

"Every employee is a hero to their own families and would not like to be demeaned in front of them."

The President was silently listening to her. He was trying to relate to the facts by thinking about the event. He was thinking about the gathering in the hall, the clapping sound coming from one end only and moreover meeting very few families. He remembered vividly that most of the employees during tea break were chatting separately in smaller groups and came up to him to wish him only and slipped off. He was mostly surrounded by Sales people throughout the event. He looked at Komal and asked her, "Do you think there is some problem in our rewarding process or managers have failed in selecting the right candidates?"

Komal did not reply to it other than uttering softly, "The list of awardees reflects the management's mindset." There was complete silence for a while. Nobody spoke. The President was looking at the wall, fiddling with his pen in his hand. "What does that mean?" he asked softly. "I mean what do you mean by organisation's mindset?" Komal thought for a while; then she decided to put her analysis in black and white to him. She believed that he was a mature person and understood things from a larger perspective. Moreover, she had felt during various interactions that he did not take things personally and listened to disagreements on merit.

She opened up, "Zero recognition is better than wrong recognition. Public recognition is a very sensitive area and is a very strong platform for promoting bonhomie by managing effectively. Employees have their own evaluation parameters. They cheer those awardees who meet their parameters. They celebrate and connect with them. Moreover, the Reward and Recognition programme is considered to be a festival. Every function and department looks up to it as an opportunity to recognise their star performers. R&R is a two-edged sword. If handled well, it works as a big engagement tool, but mishandling can lead to multiple short-term and long-term damages. While management has all the right to select the awardees, the selection should be based on facts to build credibility around it, or else many a time it ends up projecting the particular department as the 'Management' department. Like, if more awards go without any reason to the finance department, then the employees will feel the President is the *Finance* President and not the organization's head. It is easy to nominate but very difficult to nominate the right person," she ended abruptly, emphasising on the last sentence.

The President was looking at her curiously and was waiting for her to continue. He was silent but was listening to her sincerely and trying to relate. She continued, "We do recognise other functions, but our other function awards are mostly team awards." He uttered, "Yes, we have recognised and given team awards to them like Finance, HR, Security, Store, Vigilance, Security, Legal, etc. We did not miss any. We know they are contributing to the organisation, and we are thankful to them." He emphasised on the last sentence about being thankful. "Sir, by this, are we trying to convey that the management is not capable of evaluating individual performances of a larger audience? Is the organisation only capable of evaluating the easily visible metrics like number or revenue? Other organisations, globally, are able to evaluate it since decades. By this, are we not exposing our incapability?" Komal continued with the same passion but softly, "Employees of this era are sharp; they can easily see through it. Are we trying to say that it is not their problem but the organisation's challenge in evaluation capability?"

She stopped and looked at the President. He was lying back on his chair and was looking outside the window. The frown on his face was coming and going. He kept looking out for a few minutes. There was complete silence. Nobody spoke for a few minutes.

Then he broke the silence. "You have a point. The organisation is responsible for treating every employee fairly and equally. *If the organisation lacks a proper mechanism, then it's their failure.* I think we need to put two things in place immediately. Number 1: Every manager should be able to evaluate the team accurately. At least 80% of the KRAs can be measured. Plan a training programme to first *train the managers to know 'what to expect from employees and how to evaluate them.' And, Number 2: Promotions are to be made based on not only performance but also on the capability to handle a new role.* Thanks for sharing the perspective. I am totally in agreement with their expectations of rewarding the correct person."

He got up and patted Komal on the back and said, "I liked your honesty in sharing the grey areas. You chose to present it instead of sitting on it. You have played your role very effectively. The biggest contribution of HR to any manager is to 'make them think and behave like managers.' I owe you a coffee, Komal."

6

The Blind Men and the Elephant

I grew up listening to this interesting short story. It is one of the many bedtime stories shared by my grand mom when we were kids. A few of them are all-time relevant, evergreen like Dev Anand, the legendary Indian movie star.

While recollecting some stories, I find many of them to be very relevant at any stage of life, whether personal or corporate. These old-time stories are filled with management messages and learnings. One can find the link with current organisational culture and processes. Many of the characters and situations can be found around us in some way or the other, with differences in fashion or technology, while their crux remains the same. At times, they look so relevant, as if they are the real-time Ms. or Mr. X of our day-to-day lives when it comes to areas such as Team Bonding, Role Clarity, Favouritism, Succession Planning, Development Plans, Training Need Analysis, Competency, etc. One of the interesting stories from granny's bag of stories is called *Six Blind Men and an Elephant,* which is relevant even today and is worth sharing for the benefit of many youngsters who were not fortunate enough to have enjoyed these bedtime stories. This generation is largely glued to their mobile phones and laptops and interact more with apps than with the people around them. The story goes like this:

There was a village near a forest. It was so near that, very often, wild animals used to enter the village. Fortunately, none of them ever caused any damage to any human being. Generally, they were harmless. Animals used to go to the pond to drink water or play around in the water and go back. The villagers were also accustomed to finding animals in the pond and were not too concerned and did not try to put a fence around it. It was believed by village elders that these animals were harmless and they attacked only in defence.

One fine morning, an elephant walked inside the village and went to the pond to have a bath. While he was standing near the pond and enjoying the greenery around, six men came walking to the pond to have a bath. These men were blind and lived in the Blind Hostel constructed by the village community. These men used to visit the pond regularly to have a bath and spend some time together. They had been doing it religiously for ages and were doing the same that day.

One of them touched the leg of the elephant and said, "Oh, there is a big tree. I think we have come to the wrong side." The second person moved ahead from the other side and touched the tail and said, "No, brother, it seems somebody has put the rope hanging." On hearing this, the third person moved near, and on touching the huge body of the elephant, he said, "Yes, I think you are right; they have put the rope hanging on the wall," and called the other three. The fourth guy came in front of the elephant, and while touching its tusk, he yelled, "It is a slope for the kids." Meanwhile, the fifth one touched its huge ear and exclaimed, "It's a fan. Villagers have put up a big fan to cool the place; good gesture by the villagers." The sixth man touched the long teeth and yelled, "My friends, it's a sword hanging on the wall." And then they all walked down to the pond to have a bath. The story ends here, but it throws open many questions related to our mindset, our thinking, our belief, our communication, etc.

Do you think they are wrong? If yes, why? Do we face this kind of "understanding gaps" in our daily professional life? Can it be linked to our Corporate Life?

A Beautiful Connect to Corporate Life

This story is a true reflection of the Organisational Culture of "Closed Mindset." The character of the blind men represents a sect of employees engaged in delivering the same kind of job daily for a long time. They are so-called **self-designated experts** who know their job and believe that "THEY ARE THE BEST and NEED NOT CHANGE for good." They follow the same practice and routine for years although, in the current economically changing environment, organisations need to change with time either in terms of process or technology or policies. Those who fail to change are failed by Nature and Time. There are n number of references where established organisations have failed due to their unwillingness to change and move on with time.

Different interpretations made by the blind men reflect *"Believing what we see."* It's a very common characteristic found in a few professionals who believe that whatever they see is correct. This is a case of "Frozen Approach" where we choose not to see anything beyond our perceived facts. It also reflects another characteristic of "Making others believe what we see" and the rigidity of not agreeing with others.

The story also touches upon the interesting behaviour of *"Jumping to conclusions."* It is at times observed among many people, especially those who have grown internally due to spending a longer tenure in the same organisation. They tend to get used to a certain internal process and style and gradually are not well acquainted with the "developments happening outside the organisation." Here, the intent is not to challenge or dilute the benefits of loyalty or discuss the merits or demerits of it. Rather, the objective is to take the opportunity to drive the point of promoting the culture of being "Responsible for self-development." It becomes highly critical for people who stay in an organisation for long to get updated, or else they will lag behind their peers and get categorised as "Irrelevant and Outdated."

Let us also not forget that these long-tenured employees in some organisations tend to miss learning opportunities when compared to those who change jobs. The job change gives them an opportunity to learn something new from people. Hence, organisations that promote loyalty and longer tenure need to be more cautious and invest in the development of their employees.

Status Quo Syndrome: It is not very uncommon to cross such people who are "mindset-wise blind" and cannot see beyond their self-created world of wisdom. These people tend to hide behind their rigid belief of "This is IT." It reflects a deeply sunk feeling of "insecurity" to change and live under the cocoon of STATUS QUO.

Interestingly, all six were right from their own perspective but from an overall perspective were wrong since they could not relate to the larger goal. As an employee or as a manager, it becomes very important to "keep aligned to the larger goal." Goals are the most important guiding tools to keep us focused and on the right path. However, people tend to take the easy path of "short-term visibility."

Solutions for this:

Cataract Surgery: These are the bottlenecks to any organisation's growth, and the recommended solution is "Cataract Surgery." Cataract surgery is the medical terminology for enhancing the vision of a person. Here, it touches the need to change the mindset and to correct the culture.

Develop New Taste: It is recommended to follow the simple formula adopted by newspaper publishers called readership acquisition strategy. It is one of the toughest challenges to influence a newspaper reader to switch to another newspaper. Readers are addicted to the use of font, columns, size, presentation style, writing style, editorial, advertisement placing, etc., used in the paper they read. They are likely to look for the same font and same presentation in the new newspaper. Hence, to promote a new paper, **what should a new publisher initiate?** The new one could provide the customer a free trial for certain weeks or offer freebies, etc. Yes, it's done for several weeks, not days, as ironically the *brain, which is the softest part of the body, is the toughest to change!*

Create a learning environment by promoting "interaction with peers outside the organisation." Develop the learning culture by recommending **participation in seminars, conferences and talk shows**. To strengthen the best practices further, **guest speakers** from outside can be invited for more meaningful interactions. **Promote readership clubs**. It will help in learning new things

Share Success Stories: One of the best ways to create learning opportunities is to learn from each other. A time-tested, proven methodology is **success stories and experience sharing.** Follow the model of 70-20-10 with 70-20 being your own entrepreneurship ability towards knowledge acquisition.

There Are Many More Colours Other Than "VIBGYOR" Only.

7

Farmers Appointed as Military Commanders

There was a king, with a large empire consisting of around 20 provinces. Due to his sudden demise, his young son was appointed as king at the very early age of 20. The young man became the head of the kingdom overnight by virtue of his position and hierarchy even though he was not groomed or coached for it. Like many other young men of his age, the new king was very impulsive.

One day, in a cabinet meeting, it was suggested to the king to hire a few military commanders for different provinces to strengthen their security system. He decided to appoint the commanders based on his preference. The Minster of Land Revenue was one of his close confidants, and he referred three farmers for the newly created position of military commanders of their respective provinces. The minister strongly recommended the candidates by suggesting that they were highly experienced farmers with good farming history, good knowledge of geography, and, moreover, they were loyal to the kingdom and had been paying taxes timely and even in advance at times and moreover they carried lots of influence over others to deposit taxes on time. The king got convinced, as he had immense trust in his minister's judgement and appointed the farmers as the Provincial Commanders of smaller provinces located in the centre of the kingdom. Further, he directed the Minister of Land Revenue to supervise their work.

The three farmers started functioning as military commanders of their provinces. As military commanders, they were also the provincial leaders responsible for all the provincial work including revenue, farming, harvesting, agriculture, trade, road construction, etc. They had the authority to build and recruit their own army. They also had the freedom to appoint other officials to run day-to-day operations! Happily, these farmers got into action in their new role and started observing how their peers/other provinces were doing it. They realised that their peers and others, especially the border-located ones, were buying elephants and horses in large numbers to make their position strong. It was told to them that elephants and horses were good for the security of the province. So, they followed the same and bought high-quality elephants and horses.

Around six months later, these farmers went to the minister for their performance review. During the review, it was observed that their ROI (return on investment) was very high and earning was low. The minister was surprised, as others were doing better while the new ones were failing in spite of holding lucrative provinces. Post review, the farmers went back and started introspecting on the causes and felt that the expenses were high due to the high maintenance cost of elephants and horses. They immediately reported back to the minister with eureka information that the elephants and horses were wasteful expenses, which were non-productive and useless, and hence they needed to get rid of them. They further presented the following logic to convince the minister:

➤ In the last six months, the elephants & horses had not worked a single day, and they only ate.

➤ Their maintenance cost was higher than that of cows and bulls.

➤ Cows and bulls were more productive since they could be used effectively for farming.

➤ Horses and elephants when used for farming failed miserably.

➤ They could not even produce milk or cow dung that could be used for fire or selling.

The minister was convinced, and he apprised the king of the hidden but highly "wasteful expenses" and strongly recommended the need to take pro-active action and stop buying these high-cost resources.

He even went a step ahead by suggesting the need to be open to invest on low-cost resources like cows and bulls in the future in the larger interest of the country's economy. He termed bulls and cows as "low-cost, high-value and high-productive resources" as proposed by the farmers. The king was very happy and instructed all the provinces to get rid of 70% of the elephants and 40% of the horses and start buying cows and bulls to utilise them. He even rewarded the minister and the farmers for such an innovative, cost-effective idea. They were publicly rewarded and recognised as star leaders. Every provincial head was made to follow the instructions of the king to demobilise elephants and horses within the time span of four months and start procuring bulls and cows without murmuring though many of them did not agree with it from within their hearts.

The kingdom was surrounded by two neighbouring kingdoms. One of them was ruled by a strong ambitious ruler. The relationship with the neighbouring kingdoms had not been cordial for a long time. A few months later, the neighbouring ruler attacked them with the desire to expand his kingdom. He deputed a large army consisting of strong elephants and horses and a trained fleet of soldiers. The army was led by highly skilled commanders. The war lasted merely for a few days, and the young king lost his empire and had to surrender. The bulls and cows failed to sustain the fight against the horses and elephants, as they did not match their skills. The loser king's empire was taken away from him, and he was made a caretaker to govern as per the rules and guidelines of the new ruler.

Questions

➢ What is the moral of the story?

➢ How do you relate it with real corporate lives?

➢ What were the main reasons for losing the kingdom?

➢ Who according to you should be held responsible for this failure?

Recap & Analysis

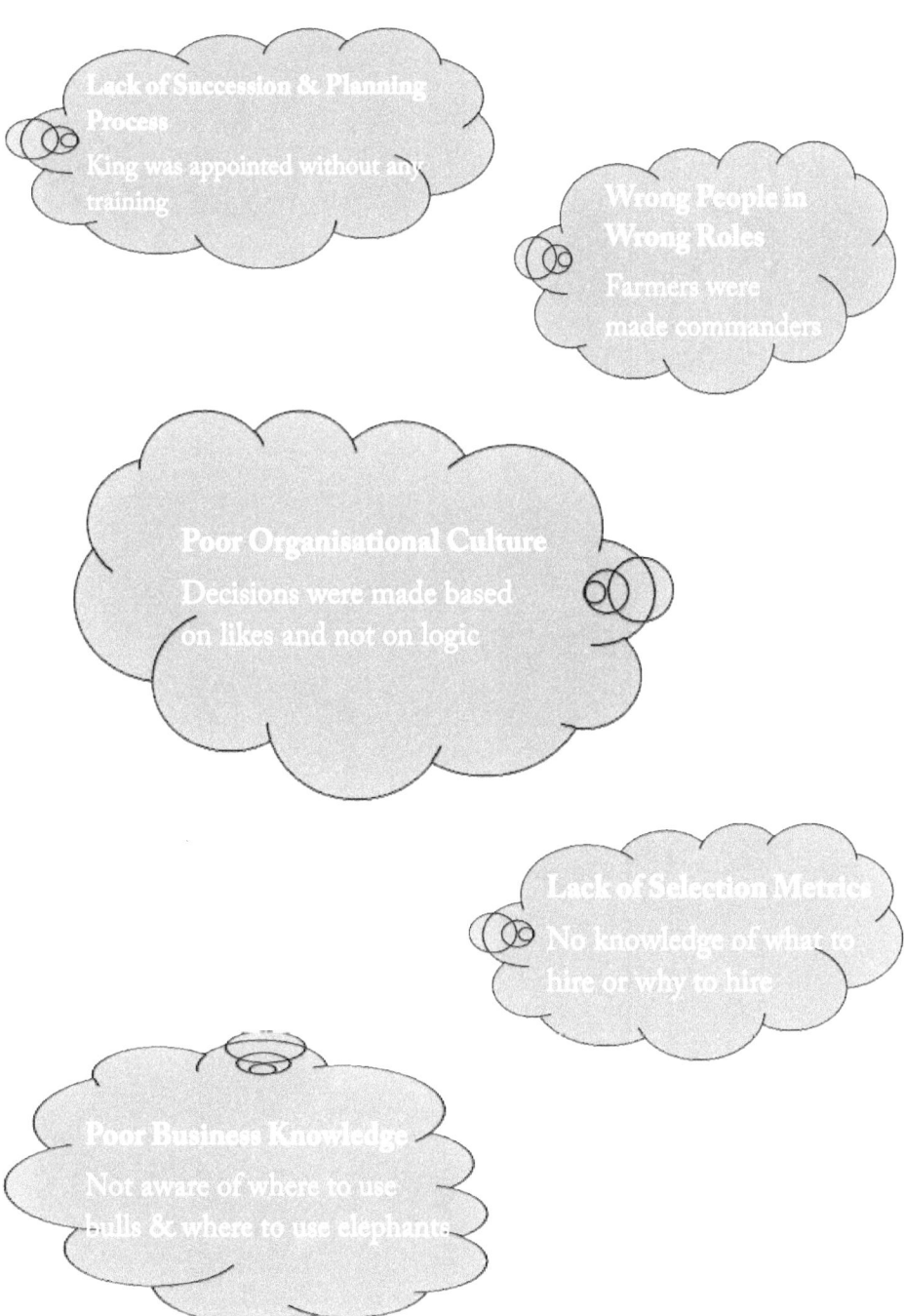

Lack of Succession & Planning Process
King was appointed without any training

Wrong People in Wrong Roles
Farmers were made commanders

Poor Organisational Culture
Decisions were made based on likes and not on logic

Lack of Selection Metrics
No knowledge of what to hire or why to hire

Poor Business Knowledge
Not aware of where to use bulls & where to use elephants

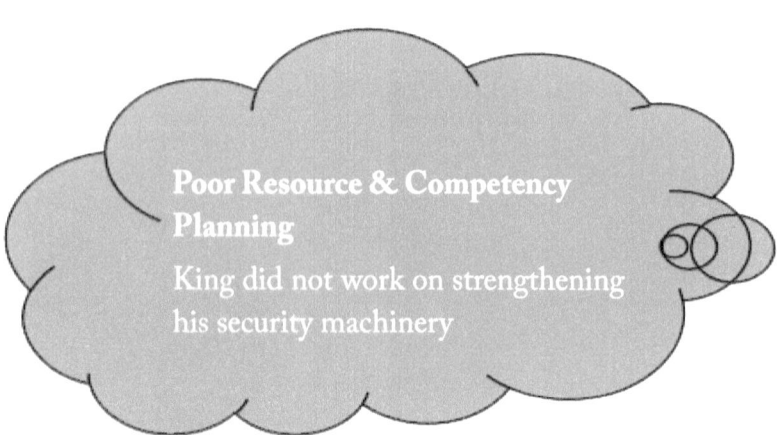

Poor Resource & Competency Planning
King did not work on strengthening his security machinery

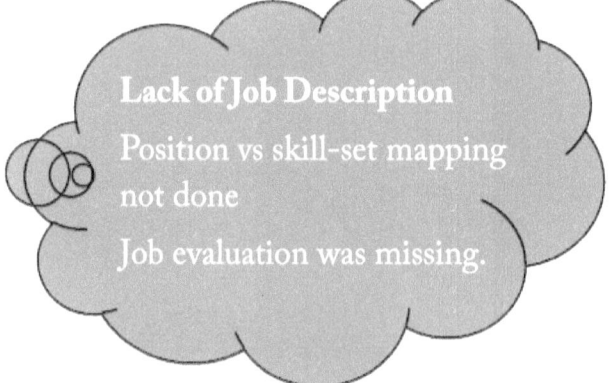

Lack of Job Description
Position vs skill-set mapping not done
Job evaluation was missing.

Lack of Vision
Lacked larger goal and futuristic approach
Lacked farsightedness

Relevance to Our Corporate World

Unfortunately, the story might sound old and historical, but its relevance can be traced in today's corporate culture. We can find these farmers and ministers and even kings in many organisations. But the most unfortunate part is the plight of the horses and elephants who are "real-time, high-potential, experienced employees" who are hired without any long-term planning, and a few organisations do not know how to UTILISE these talented, high-powered resources.

As an organisation, we need to evaluate and assess the following aspects before hiring such elephants or horses:

1. Is their role aligned to the organisation's long-term vision? (Y/N)

2. Are there defined metrics and job descriptions available in the organisation? (Y/N)

3. Is the ecosystem in the organisation ready to work with the elephants or horses? (Y/N)

4. And more importantly, is there enough competency available to evaluate and work along with the elephants/horses? (Y/N)

This is very important, as many organisations hire elephants/horses, but due to the lack of proper ecosystem and peers/superiors to utilise, they lose these people voluntarily or involuntarily. These kinds of recruitments are "influenced hirings" due to the influences of either competition, external pressures, branding exercises, etc., but soon, the euphoria vanishes, and they fail to UTILISE the elephants/horses, as they lack the right kind of peers, superiors or vision in the organisation.

The three farmers are another common type of characters found near us due to the lack of proper job evaluation and even job description. The organisations end up promoting "irrelevant skills." The promotion or growth selection metrics play an important role in building talent and a sustainable culture. These mistakes are also due to the wrong leadership in the organisation.

Succession planning is something which we all know and talk about, but very few implement it in a meaningful way. The case of weak succession planning here is an eye opener. There was no effort made by the organisation (here read as kingdom) to select the king in case of vacuum. The king is the head of the organisation, and there was a lack of seriousness observed in finding a successor for the king. Hence, the result was natural – a not-so-ready king took over the role and failed as the story unfolded.

The minister in this story was the result of poor succession planning. Wrong leaders tend to build wrong teams around them. And it has a chain influence on the culture of the organisation.

www.ingramcontent.com/pod-product-compliance
Lightning Source LLC
Chambersburg PA
CBHW021023180526
45163CB00005B/2093